DIAMOND ELITE Magazine

4th QTR Issue 2018

"A Different Type of Magazine"

Content:

Table of Content:

Pg.2 Nspire Network
Pg.3 Black Pearl Tress/Girl Best Trend
Pg.4 Divinity Devine LLC
Pg.5 Divine Treasure Box/ A Touch of Carroll/Self-Glamour
Pg.6 Destinee's Fashion/Credit Repair
Pg.7 Exotic Fantasy/Lustful Ladies Boutique
Pg.8 Soy Candles by Tasha/ MyRecipe4Life, LLC
Pg.9 Tyra Gardner/Glow Smiles LLC/Credit Repair/INV Superstore
Pg.10 Alpha Omega Theta
Pg.11 Pure Romance
Pg.12 Travel/Holistic Wellness for You
Pg.13 Angela N. Brand
Pg.14 Reality Speaks
Pg.15 Restore Build and Protect
Pg.16-17 Meet the Waltons
Pg.18 Open Positions 4 You
Pg.19 Blue Butterfly Nursing/Boutique TwoFourteen
Pg.20 The Stork Konnection
Pg.21 S365
Pg.22 Robbed of Purity
Pg.23 BossUp Networking Event

Mission Statement:

Diamond Elite Magazine's goal is to boost the exposure and sales of entrepreneurs. We believe networking and word of mouth are the biggest essentials when it comes to small business. As the years continue, we plan to thrive in success and help expand the small businesses who have contributed along the way.

Be sure to take a Photo and Contact the Small Business Owners directly if you would like to purchase a product or service! Also, visit the websites to place an order!

Tell Them Diamond Elite Magazine sent you!

Quality and Affordable Virgin Hair Extensions

Black Pearl Tress LLC

(404) 220-9297

**Why Stress?
Order Black Pearl Tress!**

f Black Pearl Tress

📷 @blackpearltress

t @pearltress

www.blackpearltress.com

Trina Necole
(310) 722-1558

www.girls-best-trend.com

@girls_best_trend   f @califigureeight

BEAUTY CAN BLING!

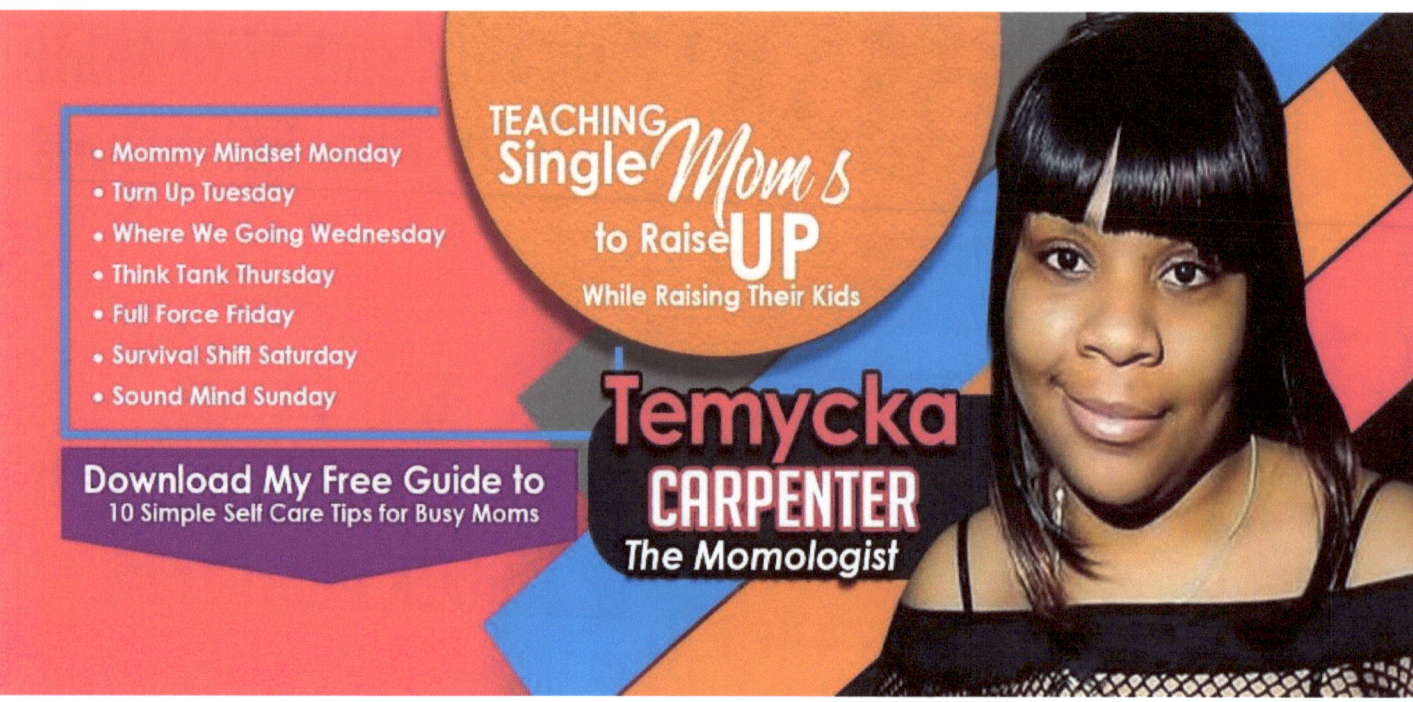

- Mommy Mindset Monday
- Turn Up Tuesday
- Where We Going Wednesday
- Think Tank Thursday
- Full Force Friday
- Survival Shift Saturday
- Sound Mind Sunday

Download My Free Guide to 10 Simple Self Care Tips for Busy Moms

TEACHING Single Moms to Raise UP While Raising Their Kids

Temycka CARPENTER
The Momologist

Divinity Devine LLC

Divinity Devine LLC is an Enterprise that crushes drama and anything that stands in our path to give our families our very best. We make a way out of no way. We are resourceful, mindful and full of life. We are on a mission to reclaim our right to self-care. Debt Freedom is our birthright, and we deserve to live a limitless life. We allow our divine femininity to guide us in becoming our best possible selves. We create the opportunities that we desire, and we are DONE wearing the supermom cape. Asking for HELP is our superpower. We bend, but we NEVER break.

Contact Details:
Temycka Carpenter (The Momologist)
Divinity Devine LLC
P.O. Box 865
White Plains, NY 10602
(914) 433-8116
Divinitydevinellc@gmail.com

- **f** @divinitydevinellc
- **◉** @single_momologist
- **t** @singlemomologis
- **in** @divinitydevinellc

www.divinestreasurebox.com
(678) 852-4335

All your unique, but fashionable items that come with the option to be creative and pick your exact colors down to the tea to fit your outfit, theme or party!

Divines Earrings are the prized possession treasure in the box. With these you may send us special instructions with colors you want, even if not listed.
Tell us what you want and it will magically appear out the box.

Divines Treasure Box
Come Pick Your Treasure

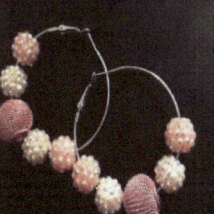

 Divines_treasurebox

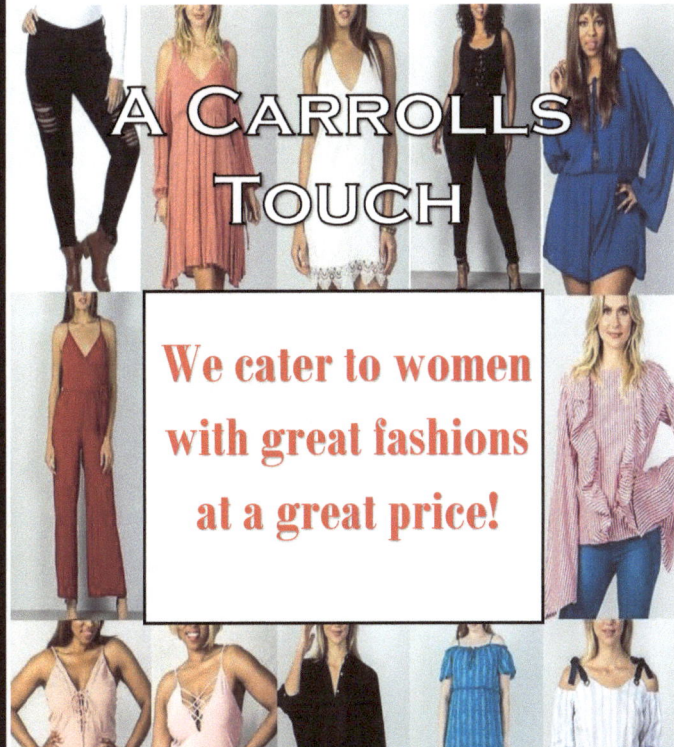

A Carrolls Touch

We cater to women with great fashions at a great price!

www.acarrollstouchofapparel.com

Self Glamour
"Bringing Your Selfies Back To Life"

www.selfglamourllc.com

f @Self Glamour @Self.Glamour

Self Glamour LLC sells hair extensions, lashes and other accessories. I, Jada Cummings, want individuals to dress up and be glammed out with Self Glamour products!

www.destineesfashion.com

@destineesfashion2

Destinee's Fashion

Destinee's Fashion

Destinee's Fashion was founded in 2016 by Larendra McDonald Spencer who is a talented and experienced seller. All the jewelry in the store comes directly from the manufacturer to bring the customers the best products at a low price. Since our establishment, we've made a promise to ourselves and our loyal customers, to continue having stunning pieces available for them to add to their collection. Which is why our loyal customers keep coming back.

CREDIT REPAIR

Restore, Rebuild, and Protect Yo
Helping Good people with Bad

Financial Education Services

AnnditaDadzie.fes@yahoo.com

WE HELP REMOVE
- ✓ Late payments Tax liens Judgements
- ✓ Medical Bills Evictions Foreclosures
- ✓ Student Loans Bankruptcy Collections
- ✓ Public Records Repossession and more!

Myfes.net/adadzie1
(919) 633-4758

Luxurious Pleasure All-in-One

Shop with Exotic Fantasy for a night filled with fun!

www.exoticfantasy.net

Lustful Ladies Boutique

www.lustfulladiesboutique.com

$10 off $100 or more

Come shop with us online!!!

Follow us on Facebook and Instagram

Lustful Ladies Boutique, LLC

317-599-2475

www.lustfulladiesboutique.com

@lustfulladiesboutique   @lustfulladiesboutique

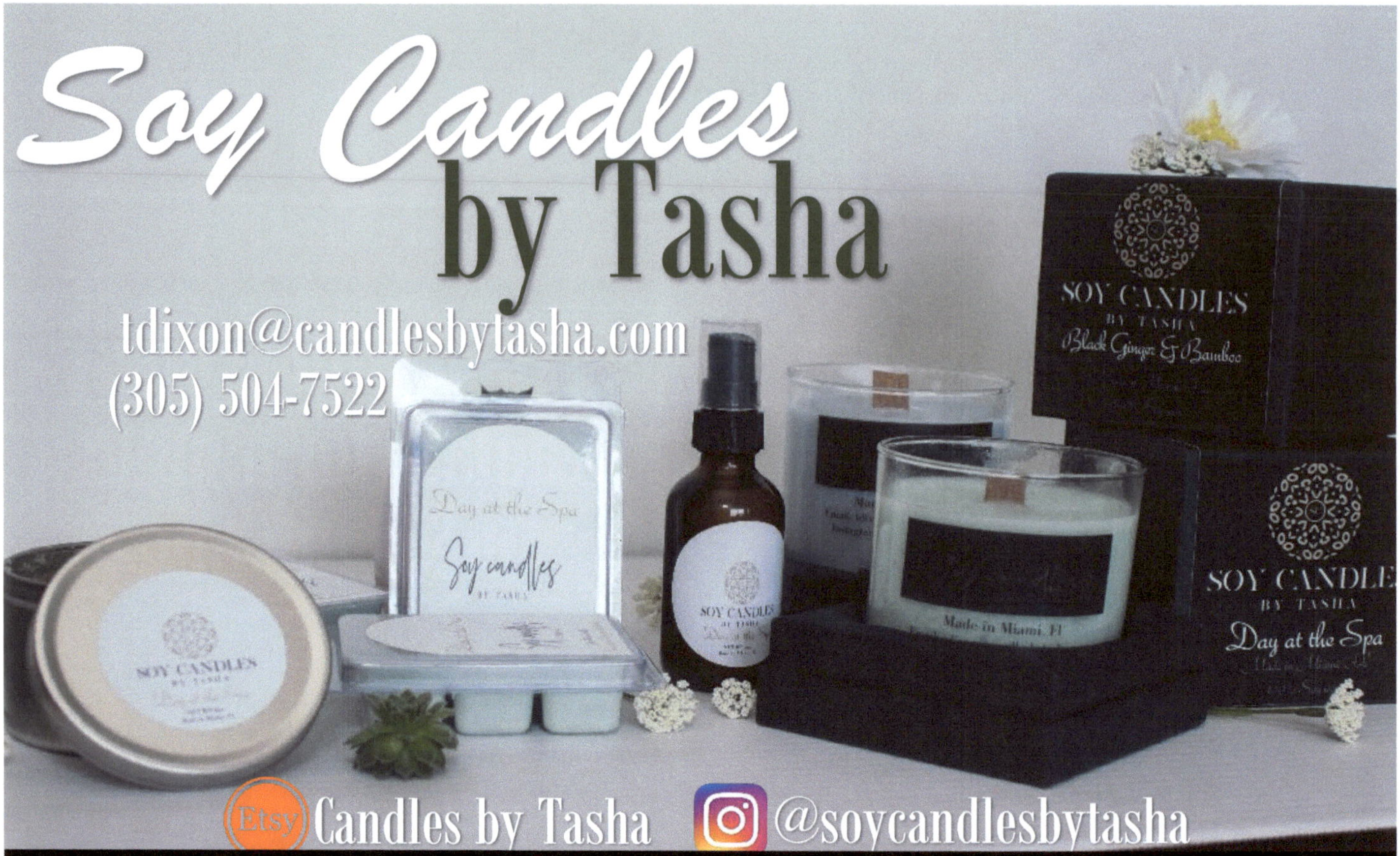
Soy Candles
by Tasha
tdixon@candlesbytasha.com
(305) 504-7522
SOY CANDLES
BY TASHA
Black Ginger & Bamboo
Day at the Spa
Soy candles
SOY CANDLES
Made in Miami, Fl
SOY CANDLES
BY TASHA
Day at the Spa
SOY CANDLES
Etsy Candles by Tasha
@soycandlesbytasha

Myrecipe4life, LLC

Love. Peace and Soulfood

www.myrecipe4life.com

Chef – Event Planner - Networker

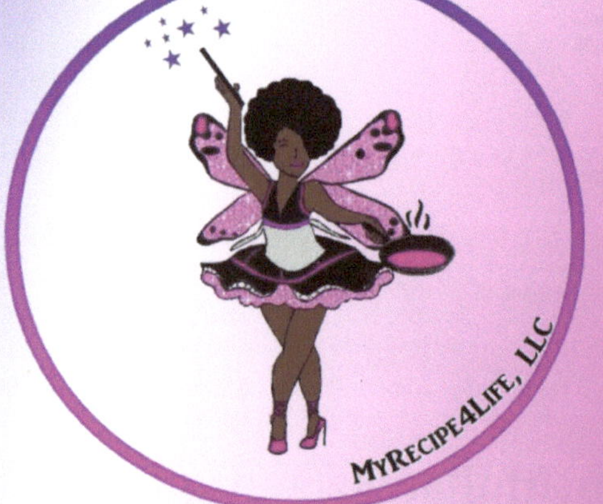
MyRecipe4Life, LLC

Ms. Tsahi Alexander – Owner/Operator
(347) 669-9363
@myrecipe4life
@myrecipe4life

Private Chef – Meal Prep – Homeade

Sauces – Spices – Rubs and Marinades

TYRA GARDNER
PsychoTherapist – Speaker - Author
(855) 855-2151
www.tyrasgardner.com

Glow Smiles LLC
Hands Free LED Whitening Kit
Cost $40.00
(618) 560-6773
Glowsmilesco32@gmail.com
Glow Smiles LLC @Glow_Smiles_LLC

IVL Credit Restoration

CREDIT REPAIR
Available In ALL States

IT'S NOT JUST ABOUT CREDIT REPAIR, IT **ALSO INCLUDE**
- WILL
- LIVING TRUST
- CREDIT ATTORNEY
- LIFE LOCK
- DEBT ZERO
- POWER OF ATTORNEY
- CREDIT MONITORING
- CREDIT BUILDER
- DISCOUNT SHOPPING
- TRAVEL DISCOUNT

WE HELP REMOVE
- BANKRUPTCIES
- FORECLOSURES
- CHARGE-OFFS
- JUDGMENTS
- TAX LIENS
- EVICTIONS
- STUDENT LOANS
- COLLECTION ACCOUNTS
- MEDICAL INQUIRIES
- LATE PAYMENTS
- PUBLIC RECORDS
- REPOSSESSIONS
- IDENTITY THEFT

Msivey1971@gmail.com

INV Superstore
www.INVSuperstore.com
Your Online Superstore for Gifts & Toys, Electronics, Bath & Body Products, Home & Garden Decor, Outdoor & Sports Equipment & more!

BIG BARGAINS   **BIG** BRANDS   **BIG** SELECTION

Free Shipping! USA & Canada
All Products, Everyday!
No Minimum Required!

Visit Us Online Today!
www.INVSuperstore.com

We accept payments via:
VISA   AMERICAN EXPRESS   MasterCard   DISCOVER

Alpha Omega Theta
SORORITY INC
EST. 2017

In the spirit of sisterhood, we serve mankind

We are the amazingly vivacious women of Alpha Omega Theta Sorority Inc! We are a non-collegiate social sorority for women in business. We are currently hosting our Fall 2018 rush! We would love for you to learn more about our sorority and what we do! Check out a call on our website, simply click on the "contact" page!

www.thetawomenunite.org

f @AlphaOmegaTheta **◉** @iamathetawoman

NEED TRAVEL?

I can help you travel the world as a V.I.P. Client or as a Paid Agent.
The Choice is Yours!
Great Deals & Great Income
Become a Travel Agent Today!

Hotels – Flights – Car Rental – Cruises

Vacation Packages – Tickets - & More

Danielle
(702) 900-6490

www.evotravelagent.com/flyyhighngetaway

Holistic Wellness For You
Helping you live your best life

www.holisticwellnessforyou.com

- **f** Holistic Wellness For You
- 🐦 @holisticwell4u
- 📷 @holisticwell4u
- **P** Holistic Wellness For You

Teaching a more constructive method of dealing with life and its stressors for individuals to be able to live their best life with signature services for addiction, recovery and relapse prevention.

Meet Angela N. Brand

f TheQueendomCoachAB

Ig @TheQueendomCoach

t @QueendomCoach

Angela Brand is a Best-Selling Author, Publisher, Master Trainer, Certified Life Coach, Powerful Empowerment Speaker inspiring individuals all over the world to "Take Ownership" of Who they Are, Where they Are, Where they Been, and Where they are Going.

She is the Founder/CEO of Queendom Life University where she trains coaches and speakers to be paid to be themselves through the AB Life Coaching & Speaking w/ Power & Passion Certification Programs.

Angela believes because of her struggle of rejection, and self-identity crisis, being molested multiple times by six different men from the tender age of 5 to 19 she was called to empower women to discover their true purpose in life by embrace their Mess as their Message.

Her mission is to make an Impact on the world through her message and motivated people to grow and reach for their highest potential.

Book Anthology & Coaching Workbook Available Now!

Order Now on Amazon or www.queendomlifeuniversity.com

Meet the Waltons

2 Entrepreneurs + 3 Kidpreneurs = 5 Waltons

When you look up the words "happily married", you would probably see a picture of the Waltons. It's not because they have not had their struggles in marriage, but because they discovered how to tap into the humor of life to keep them balanced and happy. They know that prayer really does change things and they know that married life is about building strong legacies....and yes you can be "happily married."

The Walton's aren't your typical couple; they are a power couple, winning in marriage, full-time business and ministry. They are parents to three amazing Kidpreneurs, Chris II, Kai-Milan and Winter, and they know firsthand what it means to build a successful life together. Everything they do involves one another. This was not always a happy place for them, but after maturing, fighting for their marriage, and growing together they built a chemistry that has made them unstoppable.

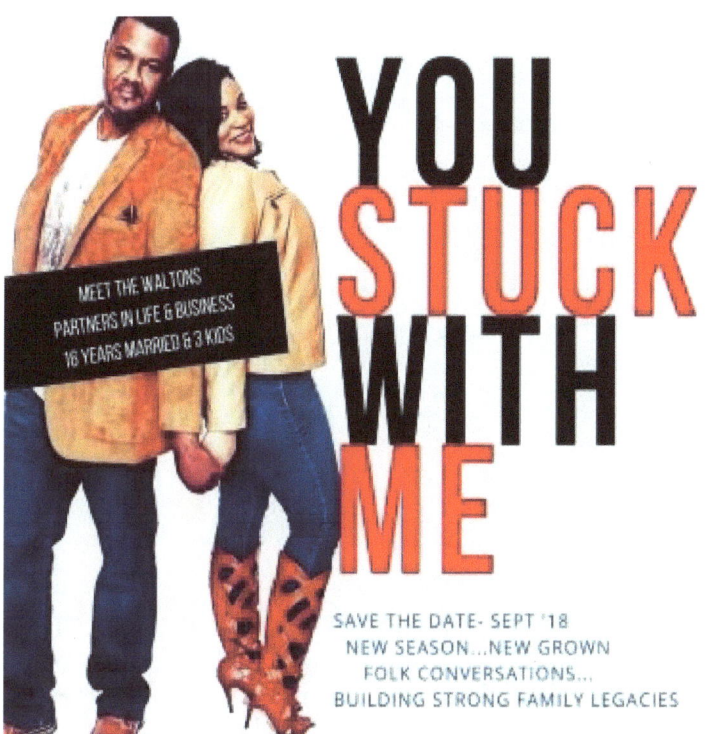

They have overcome hardships and financial difficulties, being homeless-twice, relocating and starting a new life in a new state where they knew no one and many other tragic occurrences. After successfully surviving their own trauma, they knew it was time to help build others. Their tests have become their testimony.

The Walton's travel around the world teaching men and women how to build a strong successful family unit. They provide the tools needed to heal, and restore families. They rehab relationships and create an impact that saves lives. Their 16-year marriage is a testament that marriage does work!

Some of their show/discussion topics include:

- What makes a man "not cheat" on his wife?
- Why do bad together, when you can do bad by yourself?
- Is the relationship worth saving?
- How to remain in your happy place, when all hell is breaking loose.

For more information of Booking:

Contact Mia Thomas, Publicist

(505) 402-0199

www.openpositions4you.com

We match employees to employers. We place employees with employers across the United States.

For **Business Owners**
- Candidate Sourcing
- Candidate Prescreening
- Background and Reference Checks
- Software Application Upgrades and Rollouts
- Staff Training

For **Job Seekers**
- Resume Critiquing
- Job Placements
- Software Trainings
- Skillset updating

All business' can use an extra set of hands to handle a big project or a new surge in business. We can provide those set of hands. We will find the perfect candidate for your jobs – temporary, contract, or permanent – because we know that you simply don't have the time for the full vetting candidate process. The vetting process for finding a candidate is tedious – and costly, we help you to keep those cost down. We use active and passive ways to recruit people into our talent pool.

We understand that there are many of you who are not actively looking for employment. Instead, you are waiting for "good jobs" to come to you. You are the type of candidate that we consider to be passive candidates. You have the skill sets that we need to fill the positions that we have. We are not shy in reaching out to you and creating a relationship so that somewhere down the line when we come across a position that meets your skill set and what you're looking for to make that move, we can contact you.

Blue Butterfly Nursing
Providing Medical Certification Training

I offer:
- AHA cpr
- First Aid
- mental health first aid *(for adult and youth)*
- ServSafe Food Handler and Food Manager
- CABS (child and babysitting safety)
- Phlebotomy Tech

www.bluebutterflynursing.com

Blue Butterfly Nursing @bluebutterflynurse @bbutterflynurse

Accessorize your Confidence...

Text 214 to 55469 for New Arrival

www.boutiquetwofourteen.com
628-E Wade Hampton Blvd. Greenville, SC 29609

The Stork Konnection

The Stork Konnection specializes in diaper cakes and unique diaper designs. A diaper cake is Practical, stylish, fun and elegant. Diaper cakes are perfect for baby shower centerpieces, a gorgeous hospital gift, or a charming decoration for baby's nursery.

1-800-214-9802
www.storkkonnection.com
storkkonnection@yahoo.com

Coming Soon!

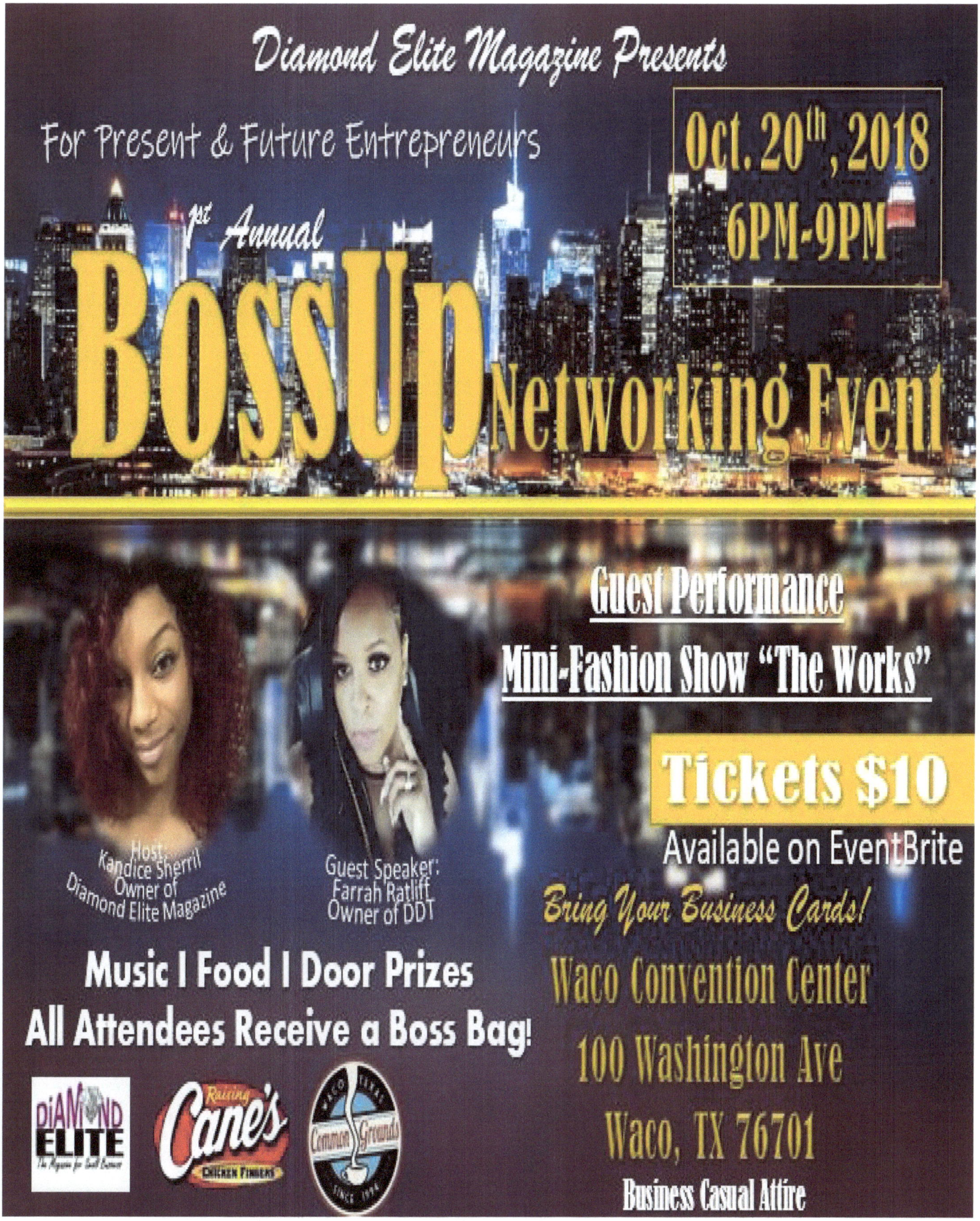
Diamond Elite Magazine Presents
For Present & Future Entrepreneurs
Oct. 20th, 2018
6PM-9PM
1st Annual
BossUp Networking Event
Guest Performance
Mini-Fashion Show "The Works"
Tickets $10
Available on EventBrite
Host: Kandice Sherril Owner of Diamond Elite Magazine
Guest Speaker: Farrah Ratliff Owner of DDT
Bring Your Business Cards!
Music I Food I Door Prizes
All Attendees Receive a Boss Bag!
Waco Convention Center
100 Washington Ave
Waco, TX 76701
Business Casual Attire
DIAMOND ELITE
Raising Cane's
CHICKEN FINGERS
Common Grounds

Need Advertising?

1st QTR Slots

NOW OPEN!

www.diamondelitemagazine.com

"The Magazine for Small Business"

www.ingramcontent.com/pod-product-compliance
Lightning Source LLC
Chambersburg PA
CBHW051836210526
45473CB00005B/1897